SALES MADE EASY

HOW WILL MY PRODUCT SELL IN MEXICO?

SANDRO PIANCONE
Chief Mexpert Officer

Mexpert [n., v. mek-spurt]:
The leading authority in doing business profitably in Mexico, relied on by some of the world's largest companies for step-by-step process and successful export of consumer packaged goods into the Mexican marketplace-without lawyers or international trade hassles, guaranteed.

ISBN: 978-1502754783
ISBN: 1502754789

TABLE OF CONTENTS

Introduction

Meet the MEXPERT

Hi my name is Sandro Piancone. I am the Chief Mexpert Officer of Mexico Sales Made Easy. And if you are wondering, yes, Mexpert is a real word: or at least it is now. I trademarked it. I am called the Mexpert for a reason. Not because I have a degree in selling in Mexico, or have a degree in international business or finance, but because I have made more mistakes than anyone reading this book, and I've spent more money making those mistakes so that you don't have to. I could write a novel just on the mistakes I have made. My team and I will make sure you and your company does not make the same mistakes that I have made over the last 14 years.

Of course while making mistakes, I also had some home runs and grand slams. Since 1998, I have generated well over 500 million dollars in sales and profits for my clients and partners helping them export their products into Mexico. That is why I titled my first book, *The Secret Treasure Map to selling your products in Mexico, and still be home in time for dinner.* My clients have found their riches in Mexico, why not you? Read on.....

Get your monthly Mexpert Report FREE! Go to:
www.mexicosalesmadeeasy.com

In my bio, it says that I am a recovering CEO of a publicly traded food distribution company in Mexico. I took an idea and turned it into the first nationwide distributor of imported products into Mexico, going from 0 to $100 million dollars a year in just under 3 years. But that is a story for another day and another book: the wounds are still too fresh.

I can't remember being as bullish about the opportunities for American companies exporting to Mexico as I am today. It's not just the dynamics of the Mexican economy itself, but with the economy doing so bad in the United States, and our government printing money like crazy, the only benefit, is that it is making our dollar weak, so that your products seem cheap to the rest of the world, including Mexico, where more than 115 million people live.

I always had my doubts about the downside of the free trade zone. Politicians that have tried to blame any weaknesses in our own economy on the mechanism of the NAFTA agreement have come and gone, but NAFTA is still here and, in fact, working tremendously well and doing what Presidents Reagan and Clinton believed it would.

One of Obama's central policies in the 2008 election campaign was taking apart NAFTA: a policy that, thankfully, has quietly disappeared.

But let's look at Mexico, and why I believe it is such a great place to do business now.

Over the last 20 years, Mexico has really started to pull its weight in the world. It's now the 12th largest global economy, and is pushing toward a top ten spot. The economy is now heavily weighted toward the services sector, and with such emphasis being placed on its education system the move toward a society reliant upon banking, finance, insurance, and retail is a given.

This in itself gives a great in for American exporters, not just of food and beverages, but also all manner of other goods aimed at a rapidly growing middle class consumer based. It's a young society, too, and one that is growing at over 1% each year. That's hardly a population explosion, but with the educational aspirations now inherent within the country, as well as the economic growth being seen now and through the future, the number of middle class consumers is likely to grow quite rapidly from the present 50 million or more. And that's a huge potential target market for all US exporters.

Indeed, as an indication of the potential growth available, you just have to look at the growth of the Mexican economy and its retail sales. Mexico suffered a pretty horrendous collapse of its economy as a result of the global financial crisis. But it's a testament to the political stability of the nation, and good economic management, that she has recovered so rapidly and continues to grow much faster than its NAFTA neighbors. You know the IMF forecasts for growth looking out two or three years puts Mexico up there with some of the fastest growth economies today. And that growth is available right on our doorstep, not across oceans and half way around the world.

I am also a fan of the way that the Mexican government has a real hand in controlling its finances. Its budget deficit and net national debt is way below that of the United States, not just in absolute terms but more importantly in terms of respective GDP. This gives the Mexican government a huge fist to wield against any future economic shocks.

Times are tough in the United States, and it looks like it's going to be tough for a long time. Taxes are rising, and government spending falling as the huge debt is tackled. Mexico doesn't face such problems. And that's good news for employment there, which is just a shade above 5%, which in turn is good news for retail sales. And that's going to encourage plenty of imports from the United States.

So, all things considered, it's a great time to be doing business in Mexico. And that brings me to talking about how you can get involved if you're not already, and if you are, how you can improve procedures and processes that will get your product across the border and to the point of sale faster and more efficiently.

I've been in business since I was a kid. I've built businesses from nothing and then sold them on as I moved to new challenges. A great part of my career history is grounded in the food and beverage business, and I've founded and grown fast food and traditional restaurant chains, as well as exporting companies. I suppose really that I was always looking for the business that presented me with the greatest satisfaction. And that's what I've found with Mexico Sales Made Easy.

So it dawned on me that there are a whole lot of businesses not only making these mistakes, but also because of them they were being held back from making real riches in Mexico. And eventually, when they did find their products in place and ready to sell, margins had been shot to shreds because of the cost of those mistakes. To me, this was a great waste. So I decided to do something about it, and founded Mexico Sales Made Easy.

CHAPTER 1

HOW WILL MY PRODUCT SELL IN MEXICO?

"Whenever you see a successful business, someone once made a courageous decision." – Peter F. Drucker

How Will My Product Sell in Mexico?

Great question! In fact, it's the million-dollar question and probably the reason you bought this book. People ask me that all the time, and I tell them stories of products that are not only selling, but also selling very well. Let me just name a few: the Maruchan Cup of Soup, prosciuttos from Italy, Monterey jack and mozzarella from California, pizzas (millions and millions of them), muffins from Canada, baby pumpkins for decoration only, and Tequila from China (yes, you heard me right, tequila from China).

After I tell these funny, but exciting stories, I ask my eager listeners about their go-to-market strategy and more importantly, their marketing plan. Yes, you can almost always get a new product on the shelf because Mexican wholesale buyers are pretty good about giving new products a shot, but you need a plan to get the consumer to take it off the shelves. That's where the magic comes in, or the real question, "How will my product sell in Mexico, more than once?"

Get your monthly Mexpert Report FREE! Go to: www.mexicosalesmadeeasy.com

A GREAT PRODUCT LOOKING FOR A NEW MARKET

So, you've got a great product. You may have started selling in your home market already. Perhaps you're testing the water, or maybe it has already established itself as a favorite among your target customer base. It might be you've put yourself on an aggressive growth path, and to achieve that you need to open up new markets. The question is, "where?"

You don't have to look any further than just across the border at Mexico. It's the second largest market for U.S. goods in the world, and, contrary to popular belief, almost half the Mexican population is middle class. The median age in Mexico is 27 – just about the age when people begin spending their increasing earnings. Of course, Mexico and the U.S. also have favorable trade terms – thanks to NAFTA. All of these factors, and more, make Mexico an ideal target market for American goods. This is something I discuss in my first book, Discover the Secret Treasure

<u>Map to Selling Your Products in Mexico and Still be Home in Time for Dinner</u>. *Have you read it yet? If not, put this down and go order it on Kindle right now, You can have it in 20 seconds.*

So now, having read my first book, you're considering entering the lucrative Mexican market. You now understand that exporting to Mexico is easier than you first thought– especially if you partner with an expert in the business – and the tax and trade concessions are pretty enticing, too.

Later in this book I'll discuss how to market, sell, and distribute your products throughout Mexico. I'll also give you a Spanish lesson (not that you'll need it), and you'll quickly learn enough of the lingo to sell and make money in Mexico. Now I'm not trying to sound like an infomercial, but there's still more! The last chapter shares a secret to help you unlock the door to up to $300,000 of free advertising. Yes, you did hear that right - $300,000 of FREE advertising!

Even now, though, you may still have a doubt. A little voice inside your head asking the same question over and over - and it's the million-dollar question, too.

First, let me assure you that the consumer in Mexico is every bit a spender as they are in the U.S. Mexicans love shopping and they love spending their money. They buy everything that other people all around the world buy – electrical goods, food, clothes, dairy products, pizza, tobacco…the list is endless. Anything you can sell in America and elsewhere, the Mexicans will also buy.

In a few moments I'll give you some examples of where we, at Mexico Sales Made Easy, have been directly involved with importation and sales successes. This includes products you might find it hard to believe could ever be sold by Americans to the Mexicans.

But first, let's look at one way you can test the water before diving in.

FOCUS YOUR EFFORTS WITH A FOCUS GROUP

Perhaps the best way to test the viability of a market is to use a focus group. This is something we help our clients with on a regular basis, and it will help you to determine several factors about the market for your product:

- You'll find out what Mexican consumers think about your product
- You'll learn what the Mexicans expect from you and your product
- You'll discover the potential size of your market
- You'll become armed with the information you need to produce a successful marketing campaign

How to get the best from a focus group

Like any research and development campaign, your focus group needs to be well planned to produce the best results. You'll need to partner with someone who knows the market place and has the expertise and contacts to gather suitable participants. Having selected your partner, you'll need to take the following steps to see the best results:

Prepare your questions/ discussion topic

Ever hear the expression, "Objection! Leading the witness" while watching a courtroom drama? That's what you have to be careful of in your focus group also. You'll need to avoid questions that seek to persuade certain responses – negative or positive.

Collect data

Don't rely on your memory – I know I can't! A suitable method of data collection will be needed, so you can record all the results – this may be audio, visual, or written.

Decide how many focus groups

Focus groups are usually limited to the number of participants and time, perhaps an hour or two at most. However, once you've decided on the agenda and exact method, then it's easy to replicate. In our experience, we have found it is extremely beneficial to do 3 focus groups on each product category. How many focus groups will you need to give meaningful results?

The advantage of focus groups

There are several advantages of using focus groups rather than individual consumer survey methods for entering a new market. To see all of these benefits you will need a skilled facilitator – the person leading the focus group discussion. But with the right facilitator in place you'll see:

- A huge amount of information inflow from participants
- Less reticence in giving that information, because of group involvement
- Real quality assessment, rather than quantity assessment – you'll understand what the Mexican buyer of your product likes about it, which will help with marketing
- The beginning of close customer relations – you'll start to be known by your target market, making the sales process even easier

Still not convinced your product will sell in Mexico?

Even with the positive results from these focus group sessions, you might still have that little voice asking you that nagging question: "How will my product really sell in Mexico?" Despite all the evidence telling you of the profitable market waiting just a few hours away, you still have that element of doubt. That's natural and you're not alone. It's the same element of doubt many exporters experience before that first profitable sale into Mexico.

SUCCESSES THAT MAY SURPRISE YOU

There are way too many success stories to tell you about now, but here's a selection of some of my favorites:

A PIECE OF CAKE

The story of **Cupcakes from Canada**: Tom Grant, a former West Jet Airlines employee, pierced the centuries old Mexican tradition of home baking and became known as 'the Cupcake Guy', or 'Chavo de los Cupcake', across Mexico. Before he took cupcakes to Mexico City, the Mexicans hadn't even heard of cupcakes. Now they sell in the hundreds of thousands.

Then there are the many success stories where Mexico Sales Made Easy had direct impact on a product's success. I've picked out just a few of these to discuss with you here.

MILKING PROFITS FROM MAGIC STRAWS

What about the story of Queso Nery's **Monterey Jack Cheese**? The company had a hugely successful sales record with their star product. In fact, its Puro Monterey Jack was – and still is – the number one selling Monterey Jack in Baja, California: its home market. Now 30 years old, Queso Nery's has become the market leader for imported cheese from the United States. Not content with this, however, Queso Nery's is continually looking for new products to market to Mexico.

Its latest is 'Popotes Mágicos' (Magic Straws) a milk straw that offers flavor without sugar (in a country that is obsessed with sugary products). This product came about because the company's management, who all has little kids, saw this great product that was flying off the shelves in a Wal-Mart in California. Each straw contains just 17 calories, and it doesn't need to be refrigerated. So, a product that kids love, and that parents want to buy because of the health benefits, with a long shelf life, it was an easy decision.

Having tracked down the manufacturer in Hungary, Queso Nery's gave us the task of taking the project from inception all the way through to the refrigerator door (more about that in a moment).

We chose the name with Queso Nery's blessing, and then made sure all the correct trademarks were secured in Mexico. We buttoned down the duties payable on the product, obtained the correct HS classification – not an easy task, especially as the chocolate flavored straw was considered completely different to the others (I have no idea why) – and designed all of the labeling.

Whew, that's a lot of details! You may think this was the end of it, but only then could we obtain the necessary PROFECO approval for the Popotes Mágicos to be displayed in stores.

But none of this would have been achievable if we hadn't showcased the product at ANTAD (Latin America's largest trade show) and conducted a 100-store mom and pop test. From those groups we discovered the packaging was all-wrong – it was too tough for kids to open. So the packaging was redesigned, and the right sales location targeted – right in front of the milk door on in-store refrigerators. The product is about to take the market by storm, with orders from the top chains across the country.

And this isn't the only thing we've been able to help Nery's with. It used to have trucks stuck at the border crossing for days and weeks at a time, as contents were checked against paperwork strewn with errors. We took Nery's whole product list, cross-checked all NOM classifications, and reclassified where necessary. We then worked with border control to ensure paperwork was "fit-for-purpose." The result? No more hold-ups. Time and money saved, and products to store shelves more quickly. What a relief!

Here's what Jose Sierra, the Brand Manager of Queso Nery's has to say about the project:

"We couldn't have launched Popotes Mágicos without Mexico Sales Made Easy. Nom 51, HS Classification and Trademark regulatory compliance is critically important for a new product — as important as milk is to cheese. We only had one shot to get it right and they ensured we were well prepared. Popotes Mágicos has been extremely successful and the Mexico Sales Made Easy team played an instrumental role in this success."

IMPORTS ARE SMOKING

We've been working with **US Tobacco De México** for a couple of years now. We started off by helping with the import of name brand and private label cigarettes and cigars into Mexico. Now, the company has opened a plant in Mexico, helping to increase their business even further.

I first met the company's VP of Private Label Distribution, Carlos Varela, at ANTAD, where we started talking about the cigarette importation market. It became clear pretty quickly that we could help his company with their importation goals: we already had some expertise in the market, particularly with fees, taxes, and logistics. The company needed more efficient distribution, and I knew we could deliver.

The company's partnership with Mexico Sales Made Easy has seen 50 trademarks filed and the complicated process of importing tobacco from America simplified beyond all recognition. That has all helped toward increasing sales and profits. But we didn't stop there.

We took care of all the regulatory headaches, the legal stuff, and the accounting laws and permits – not just for the import business, but for the recent opening of the new plant. Talk about logistics and paperwork! But we love it and we see it as an obstacle course we've navigated many times before.

Because of our connections, we were able to link US Tobacco De México with the right machine manufacturers, complete all the paperwork in a timely fashion, and ensure the project remained on track throughout.

Now the company is way ahead of its original business plan.

Carlos Varela has this to say about our working relationship:

"It doesn't have to be difficult as long as you find the right people to help you. It was a comfort to me to know MSME had already done what I needed to do. It is not complicated when you are guided by someone who has been where you are and knows all of the steps, and has the best contacts."

Yahoo! Another successful collaboration! I love it!

CHEESE: MATURING A BUSINESS

Popotes Mágicos was not my first experience with Queso Nery's. Indeed I've worked with the company for several years. I have a lot of experience in the food industry, including importation and exportation of cheeses. So it was probably natural that Queso Nery's Distribution VP, Jose Sierra, approached me with a problem he had a while back.

The company wanted to launch some new products but didn't have the expertise to complete all the necessary paperwork and legal documentation. It was important to the company to get its new cheese lines to market as quickly as possible, so we took on the work of trademarking the new lines, securing the correct HS classification numbers, and ensuring the NOM 51 labeling met approvals.

The company knew we could handle this after the way we had helped it previously. When we first started working together, Queso Nery's was having big problems with cheese imports getting stuck at the border. Numbering and packaging was wrong, and documentation incomplete. We took on the responsibility for correcting all of these problems, and within weeks the cheese was rolling smoothly. So the company knew we were more than capable of doing everything necessary.

But it's not only time we've managed to save our client. By correcting import permits and labeling, it has seen thousands of dollars in savings.

Here's what Jose Sierra has to say about working with Mexico Sales Made Easy:

"...we consider them a true partner. We meet on a weekly basis to discuss sales and marketing strategy. I can tell you, you do not get this from your average attorney or customs agency. Their experience in the cheese field is outstanding... we are very happy with the company. We would recommend them to other companies wishing to do business in Mexico, especially if you are in the cheese business."

Given such wide and varied success, it's easy to see there's really only one answer to the question of whether your product will sell in Mexico or not. That answer is a resounding 'yes'.

The Mexican consumer market is alive and kicking, stronger than ever.

Of course, there are hurdles to overcome. Just like when you first sold products in your home market. Our experience, and those of the clients who have worked with us, is not a single one of those hurdles are insurmountable. Getting your product to Mexican consumers will open a new and expanding market to you.

If I had more time, I'd tell you about the market created in Mexico for prosciutto; Calrose rice imported from California and the growing seaweed products market (even though Mexico is one of the largest seaweed producers in the world), among many other stories of imported product markets in Mexico that you wouldn't believe could exist.

But right now, it's time to tackle another important part of doing business in Mexico. Your product will sell. The market is there for it. The next question that needs to be answered is that of marketing and selling to your new, and soon to be excited, customers.

CHAPTER 2

HOW TO SELL AND MARKET YOUR PRODUCT IN MEXICO?

"There is only one boss. The customer. And he can fire everybody in the company from the chairman on down, simply by spending his money somewhere else."

- Sam Walton

THE HARDEST AND MOST FORGOTTEN PART OF BUSINESS

In my first book _Discover the Secret Treasure Map to Selling Your Products in Mexico and Still be Home in Time for Dinner_, I discussed the packaging and labeling of your product for the Mexican market, and adhering to the rules and laws so your product isn't stopped at the border. These delays can add days or weeks to your product sales cycle, as well as a bunch of costs that destroy your margins.

Get your monthly Mexpert Report FREE! Go to: www.mexicosalesmadeeasy.com

As any successful author will tell you, writing a book and then producing a great eye-catching cover is only part of the selling process. Most unsuccessful authors fail to realize the importance of marketing and selling their book, thinking that once it has been written and packaged it will sell itself. A book is 10% writing and 90% marketing. Having been a first-time author I can tell you how painful it is to come to this realization. But after a few months, we are proud to say we became a #1 Amazon Best Seller in our category. All thanks to having a marketing plan and executing it.

The same thing happens in business. If you believe you've done all the hard work by manufacturing your product and making sure it conforms to Mexican packaging laws, think again. Now that the hard work begins. This is why a great deal of our focus is on helping companies not only get their product to market in Mexico, but also sell it.

BUILDING A BRAND ISN'T EASY

In my first book _Discover the Secret Treasure Map to Selling Your Products in Mexico and Still be Home in Time for Dinner_, I discussed the importance of trademarking your name and product in Mexico. If you have not done it yet, put the book down and go to www.mexicosalesmadeeasy.com/freetrademarksearch

and let us see if your name is available. It may be already too late. This is the number one thing you need to do before you can begin building your brand in Mexico, or for that matter, anywhere in the world, including the United States.

Innumerable products – all of which should have succeeded – have failed because the companies that manufactured them didn't follow through. They got everything right. They created a great product. They produced eye-catching (and legal) packaging. They negotiated over all the customs hurdles. They got their product into warehouses. Then they sat and waited, expecting their product to sell itself.

It's only at this point they finally realize a piece of the jigsaw is missing. They created a product, but failed to produce a brand.

Anyone who has been in the business of selling knows it takes hard work and effort to build a brand, not only in Mexico but anywhere. There are so many people involved—distributors, salespeople, and consumers – that it is essential to have a marketing plan. It's like a roadmap. Without a plan, you, and your product, will get lost in Mexico. You'll be left hoping your target market finds you, rather than presenting yourself to your target market.

BUILDING YOUR MARKETING PLAN

In order to market effectively, the last thing you'll want to do is take a scattergun approach. So the first concept of effective marketing is to identify your target market. It's likely you've already done some of this work. Certainly, by using focus groups as discussed in Chapter 1 you'll be in a better position to understand who your end buyers will be.

A marketing plan is essential for doing business. You'll need to identify the best channels and methods to build your brand, and you'll need to budget accordingly. Remember, cost will be both money and time. Creating a nationwide brand is not going to be cheap; and you'll have to foot the bill. (By the end of this book, though, you'll have found out how you can benefit from hundreds of thousands of dollars of free advertising to help you on your way.)

Having a well-designed and considered marketing plan will help you keep your costs down to a minimum, but, perhaps more importantly, will present you as a true professional to distributors, retailers, and consumers. It will win you the hearts and minds of all of your target market.

The need for a marketing plan cannot be underestimated. By partnering with Mexico Sales Made Easy, you'll find we'll help with this plan, ensuring it's targeted and cost effective. You know your product. We know Mexico.

Essential elements of your marketing plan include:

- Your budget
- How you will support distributors
- How you will support retailers
- How you will reach out to your target consumer

Step 1 – Your Website

An essential part of any business today is the website. Your customers will expect you to have one, as will the shops, supermarkets, and businesses that will be selling your goods. People expect to be able to find you online, and, while you won't need to speak too much Spanish to do business in Mexico, you'll want to be represented as a Mexican-friendly business. That means you'll have to have a Spanish language version.

You'll also need to populate your website with good, informative articles or blog posts that speak to your customers.

Great example: Please visit the website of Queso Nery's (www.quesonerys.com) one of our clients, as you will see, it has all the products they carry, with recipes and videos on how to use their product, they also have their Television commercials, and info on how to order the product from the distributors located throughout Mexico. It is a great example of an interactive website.

Another great example is the Mexico Sales Made Easy website. It has a lot of educational materials, plus videos, articles, and blogs. It is very interactive too. Visit www.mexicosalesmadeeasy.com

Passive and Active Marketing

Your marketing plan should allow for both passive and active marketing of your product.

When you passively market your product, you'll be anticipating customer needs and allowing them to find you. The most relevant passive marketing is, perhaps, the website, but later we'll also look at tradeshows and how you can use them to market your products effectively to distributors and retailers.

Other marketing efforts require a more hands-on approach: networking with other businesses, and selective advertising to drive your product sales to your target market. Active marketing is deliberate and purposeful. You'll need to get out and meet your retailers and customers face-to-face. Let them know why they need your product, and what makes it better than competitor products. Doing this requires skill and persistence. For the remainder of this chapter, we'll concentrate mostly on the active marketing proposition.

POINT-OF-SALE MARKETING

Getting out and reaching your customers and buyers is the most effective marketing you can do. Point-of-Sale (POS, sometimes called Point of Purchase, POP) marketing is all about communicating your message to the end consumer, distributors, and retailers.

If I could be in every store, next to every one of our customer's products, marketing the heck out of it, I would. I love selling. I love talking to customers and sharing the excitement I have for the products. Buy I can't and you can't. That's why you need Point-of-Sale marketing.

Here are a few:

- Pop-up-displays
- In-store specials
- Tasting sessions
- Posters
- Signs
- 3-D cut-outs

All of these things communicate to the customer. They help get your message out at the exact moment it matters most – the point at which the customer makes a decision to buy. Essentially, all of this falls under the category of in-store promotion and advertising.

You might also consider special in-store events, information updates, and reiteration of the benefits of your products.

POS materials have huge potential to sell your product. It is your salesman in the store, telling your target customer to 'buy me!' Exterior advertising, such as billboards, certainly have their place, but by going in-store your advertising will work even harder for you. Billboards are seen when your customer is in a car, cycling, or walking. They help increase awareness, and keep your product talked about. But POS marketing sells better.

When your advertising is in-store, the customer can look at your product, touch it, feel it, and smell it. Your POS material can tell the customer why they should be buying your product. All your POS material will be produced to tell the customer what your product is, what it does, why it is better than competitor products. This will create a compelling case to 'buy me'.

Go spend some time in a store, and watch the products that fly off the shelf. Those that have POS marketing move faster. They sell better. Customers are drawn to them. Other similar products remain on the shelf, unless the customer has come in especially to buy those specific products.

Good POS materials

Customers will look at your POS materials and directly associate with the quality of your product. Not surprisingly, your competitors will consistently try to take down your POS materials. So will in-store staff, as they refresh displays. It is up to you to make your POS material not only compelling to the consumer, but also to the retailer.

First, be aware that your POS will be moved and removed by competitors, going in-store and replacing with their own. It's all part of the game. So you'll be faced with a continuous cost, possibly of replacing it and most certainly of putting it back up.

By designing eye-catching and good quality POS material, you'll be persuading the retailer to treat your advertising more favorably than your competitors. They'll also take care of it, meaning less cost for replacement. If you create really great POS materials, you'll begin to find they become a product in themselves, with other retailers looking to 'stock' your POS items to aid their own in-store sales.

Retailers love great advertising that draws customers into their store. And they love it even more when it's free.

Your well designed, well made, POS materials may cost a little more at the start, but they will save you a fortune going forward. Retailers take care of good POS

THE IMPORTANCE OF MERCHANDISERS IN MEXICO

Every retailer will ask if you have merchandisers, you may ask what is a merchandisers, there are a few official descriptions, and then my answer.

What exactly is merchandising?

Mexperts Answer: You can sell the product, deliver to the warehouse or the back of the store, you get all excited and come back the next week, and the product is still sitting in the back of the store.

You need to have your own merchandisers who take the product from the back of the store and put it on the shelves. If not, it will sit there for weeks, and the buyer will tell you to come pick it up, because it did not sell. Really?????

According to the American dictionary, merchandising is the activity of promoting the sale of goods at retail.

Merchandising activities may include display techniques, free samples, on-the-spot demonstrations, pricing, shelf talkers, special offers, and other point of sale methods. According to American Marketing Association, merchandising encompasses "planning involved in marketing the right merchandise or service at the right place, at the right time, in the right quantities, and at the right price."

Wikipedia says that in the broadest sense, merchandising is any practice which contributes to the sale of products to a retail consumer. At a retail in-store level, merchandising refers to the variety of products available for sale and the display of those products in such a way that it stimulates interest and entices customers to make a purchase.

To have merchandisers or not?

This is something you´ll have to answer yourself. Ultimately, depends on what is your brand's goal, and of course budget!

Want your products to stand out from your competitors? Consider hiring merchandising services. Merchandising can offer a unique competitive advantage.

If you ask me, I definitely would use merchandisers for my brands, have been using them for more than 14 years and have had all kind of experiences, good and bad.

Many people wonder how merchandising can make your company and brands a success story when the economy is not doing so great. Well, finding the right company at the right price that can provide merchandising services for your products and new items that are coming out to make sure they are placed in the stores in the proper places, is a good start.

A person who performs retail merchandising will go into a business such as Walmart, and either put out product or make sure the product has been placed in the proper place. Plus, the product must have the proper layout or schematic which is provided by the retail merchandising company.

This is a very competitive industry and there is a lot more to it than just shopping for a living. The company you finally choose, will have a lot of responsibility on their shoulders as the fate of the business can hinge on them picking the right products, merchandising them correctly and managing the stores well enough to keep customers coming back for more.

On the budget side, not always the most expensive agency is the best, that´s why I mentioned before to "wisely use your budget".

Here are some dos and don'ts when it comes to hiring a merchandiser's agency:

Dos

1. Have a pre-established budget and try not to exceed it.
2. If you're going to go nationwide, go for local agencies per state, do not hire agencies that tell you they cover the whole country, it is a complete lie, you'll waste your time and money.
3. Hire small to medium size agencies, big ones have too many companies under their umbrella, plus they have the biggest ones like Unilever, P&G and similar large companies, and would not pay the attention you want for your brands.
4. Ask the agency for a short, middle and long term plan with goals on gaining shelf spaces and total market share as well.
5. Ask the agency for weekly reports with performance's goals.
6. "Pamper" promoters, sometimes offering monetary stimulus in order to get exhibitions for free at sales floor, they are cheaper and more efficient than negotiating them at headquarters with chains buyers.

Don'ts

1. Do not put all the responsibility on the agency, you need to have an "insider" making sure they're performing the way you want, so go ahead and consider in your budget a "supervisor's supervisor".
2. Don't base your company decisions on electronic apps, like CRM for instance. You can mix both, cybernetic and human data, but I strongly suggest you to be at sales floor "breathing" what is happening there, might sound like old school, but it works.
3. The most common mistake is not doing enough merchandising, including no ticketing, no naming or just not big enough. A little bit of tinsel at Christmas time doesn't sell, it has to look generous. The opposite is also true: some companies have too many signs and tickets and too many discounts and specials on their brands. It's important to get a balance.

So remember, merchandising is the key to getting your product out of the back of the store and on to the shelves.

It determines which items are purchased, and whether a customer has a good experience that will lead to a long-term relationship, good merchandising will always deliver revenue.

Having your POS material displayed is only part of the picture. A poster can only go so far in promoting your product. If that poster is taken down every couple of days, to be replaced by a competitor, its usefulness recedes. This is where it pays to spend time, money, and effort with retail staff themselves.

Wine and dine managers. Smooth talk the salesmen. Spend time discussing your product, its merits, and how it can be best sold to customers. One of your prime responsibilities as a marketer is to make sure you get prime position at the POS. There are several things you can do to help you ensure this.

Have sales people come to your plant

Sales people rarely get treated to a day out. If you do this, you'll be putting yourself in prime position to be the preferred product of recommendation. Use a day at your plant to walk salespeople through the process of production, packaging, and to meet your people. They'll love you for it.

But don't forget, this is also an ideal opportunity to provide sales training to the people who will be selling your product. They'll know the words you want your customers to hear, see the benefits themselves, and be better informed to talk to their customers about your product.

Put yourself in this position: you're standing in front of a dozen people and have been asked to talk about something. Would you rather talk about a subject you are given, or one in which you consider yourself more than knowledgeable? I've seen sales people asked by customers about a specific brand, and that customer bought a different brand solely because the salesperson knows more about one than the other.

The retailer will love you for this, too. It provides them a free way to treat their staff, provides free training on product sales, and helps in-store morale. With absolutely no expense to them! Don't you just love a win-win? Especially when it's a fun day for everyone and long term investment in your future sales.

These days can be arranged for single companies, with staff from several stores, or even for staff from several retailers.

Take sales people to lunch

Often, salespeople may not be able to get away for a whole day. But there's nothing stopping you from taking a salesperson to lunch. This is a small price to pay for the loyalty it will build toward your product. But remember, the lunch is to help the salesperson sell your product. Have a message to give.

Ask the salesperson about competitor sales and for his or her advice on positioning of your POS material. They will respond positively, because you're showing you value them and their opinion.

Contests

You can wrap this direct in-store staff interaction into contests based on sales numbers.

Challenge stores or individual salespeople to sell your product. Point out how your POS material will help them achieve sales targets. Be prepared to offer sales training to store staff: you'll get better buy-in from management. They will have a free training session for staff. You will know your product is being sold how you want it to be.

The prizes you give for these contests will depend on the level of contest. For example, a single store contest will not produce the revenue return that a regional multi-store contest would. At the high end of the scale, a national sales contest for a major chain will warrant a major prize – perhaps a paid-for team building weekend for the winning store.

To build your brand you'll need to market your product well. To do this, you'll need to first produce a marketing plan. This will help you identify:

- Support you need to give distributors and retailers
- Methods of reaching your target customer
- Costs of doing this work

A marketing plan will start with an executive summary, just like your business plan, and include information about your product. This may include:

- Photos
- Price points
- Dimensions
- Look
- Advantages over similar products

This plan will also include your budget for marketing and brand support, and may well be detailed at levels down to sales channel, region, retailer, and distributor. This detail helps solidify return metrics – for example, cost of promotions versus return given – and serves as a roadmap to follow.

Pricing details shouldn't be only the price to the customer, but also the cost of product to you, the distributor, and the retailer.

Don't forget to include information about your competition. This will help you figure out your strategy to compete.

This might sound like a lot. That's because it is. But it is essential to do, if you want your product to be successful in Mexico. It's also an area in which Mexico Sales Made Easy has huge exposure, experience, and expertise.

We help our clients build out their marketing, target their customer, find best-fit distributors and retailers, throughout the process. We also help ensure their marketing and POS materials are presented in correct Spanish.

We also have excellent – maybe unrivalled - access to the best passive marketing tool in Mexico today. That's where I'd like to take you next, as we discuss tradeshows as a marketing tool.

A great reading recommendation: It is from one of my mentors, Dan Kennedy, The No BS Guide to Brand Building, which is a great read for all of our clients and readers of this book. A special treat, myself and my company were featured in this book, page 95-96. To order now, go to www.amazon.com

CHAPTER 3

HOW TO PROFIT FROM TRADE SHOWS IN MEXICO

"Nothing can add more power to your life than concentration all of your energies on a limited set of targets."

-Nido Qubein

BE ACTIVE AT TRADE SHOWS

In the last chapter, I briefly discussed the difference between passive and active marketing. Active marketing is more intense, requires more time, and is generally more expensive than passive marketing. This said, it also has the best results.

Get your monthly Mexpert Report FREE! Go to:
www.mexicosalesmadeeasy.com

Some marketers would consider passive and active marketing to me similar to 'pull-me, push-me' information. In simple terms, pull-me information is that acquired by someone who wants that information – for example an Internet search – and push me is where the informant pushes the information onto the target – for example, advertisements appearing on your computer screen.

Clearly, the more active the marketing the wider the audience reached. However, there is one form of passive marketing that has the capacity and the likelihood to reach millions – albeit, mostly indirectly.

Jorge Olsen, the President of Premier Brands Inc., considers passive marketing as the way of getting Mexican businesspeople to find you. He says that 'you have to make sure your products are in trade shows. You don't have to go yourself, maybe one of your customer sells at trade shows or you hire a broker that goes to trade shows.'

The beauty of trade shows is, of course, that your target market is represented by the buyers who can help take your products to your target market.

THE BIGGEST MISTAKE MADE AT TRADE SHOWS

When I first started in this business, I was really dumbfounded by trade shows. They never seemed to give the often-anticipated return on investment. The more I went to trade shows, the more I heard similar stories from participants. Money was spent – thousands of dollars, sometimes tens of thousands of dollars – without any real business being signed.

Yet at the same time, I witnessed the ink drying on contracts that saw new products being exported from the United States to Mexico. Those products were no better than others, and yet there I was, missing out on these lucrative lines of business.

It took me three years or more to eventually realize the mistake I was making. In fact it's the mistake that most product manufacturers make at trade shows. I was failing to prepare. Oh, of course, I had great displays. I had fantastic on-desk literature. I had my product briefs all figured out and rehearsed for when a prospective buyer approached our stall. The kind of preparation that is absolutely necessary, but won't cut the mustard when it comes to selling at trade shows.

That one phrase is the key to how to work trade shows for a real return on investment: don't rely on buyers buying, but get out there and sell. The only way to make a real return on your investment in a trade show is to sell to the buyers that are there.

Your opportunity is having all those buyers in one place at one time. Your problem is how to sell to them.

ACTION AT ANTAD

The solution to this problem, and the key that unlocked the tradeshow opportunity, finally came to me during ANTAD one year. ANTAD is the largest tradeshow in Mexico, with over 2,200 suppliers and 37,000 visitors gathered under one roof. It is, literally, a massive opportunity to get a foothold in the lucrative Mexican market.

I'd been participating in ANTAD for three years, with little success. Then everything suddenly clicked into place. That was the year I decided to be proactive at trade shows. Rather than set up a stand and hope for passersby to stop and hear what I had to say, I went out to them.

This is now the approach we take with our clients exhibiting at trade shows. It's so successful that I can put an almost exact figure on the return a client will expect to see from their investment. But it's hard work.

The process starts months before, with a client meeting to establish aims. Then we get down to the details of making sure those aims become reality. Gone are the days of sitting at the booth and 'accidently' signing customers. We set client appointments way in advance, sending out direct mails and emails, and backing this up with phone calls to invite potential buyers to the booth.

By the time the show comes around, we already have a diary full of buyer appointments, having confirmed them by reminder four weeks before the show, and a courtesy call the day before the appointment.

Then the client comes along to the booth at the show, we display new products, offer a free gift, and get direct contact information. By the end of the show, not only will we have signed new buyers for our clients, but also have a diary full of contacts for them.

PRESENTING AT TRADE SHOWS

The Expo ANTAD, held at Guadalajara, comes around every March and is Mexico's largest tradeshow. In fact, it lays claim to being the biggest of its kind across all of Latin America.

Many American exhibitors are reticent to take part because of the language barrier. After all, it's hard enough selling in their own country where English is spoken naturally, never mind a foreign country where Spanish is the natural language. But let's put this potential barrier to one side, because I'll discuss this in the next chapter.

First, let's look at the things you must do if you want to be successful at trade shows. We've already spoken about preparing by lining up known buyers – and the on-the-ground knowledge of a broker will prove invaluable with this process – but that will count for nothing if the other basics aren't covered.

Prepare your stand

The first thing needed is a stall that is fit for purpose. You'll need to purchase your stand – the easy part – and design your exhibition stall around it. Of course, it is possible to do all of this work remotely. However, you need to rely on your advertising, flyers, and other promotional materials reaching the venue on time. Don't forget, they'll all have to be prepared in perfect Spanish.

Samples of your product will need to be transported across the border, and pricing of goods will need to take into account any and all duties and taxes that will be levied. Then, of course, you'll need to affix proper labels on your samples.

You'll probably also want to employ the services of a translator for the major buyer that comes along and only speaks Spanish.

THE MSME ANTAD CEO TOUR

It's probably time I told you a little more about our annual ANTAD CEO tour.

This tour is something we started a few years ago, and it proved so popular (and valuable) that it has since become an annual event. The common theme for our CEO tour: great accommodations, extensive and valuable information, relaxed atmosphere, fabulous meals and exceptional tequila! Now, for the details!

We start with all delegates treated to lunch in San Diego with an afternoon preparation seminar before heading off for dinner. The following day, delegates are taken to Guadalajara by Aeroméxico. After landing, we all board a special air-conditioned limo-bus which takes us to a local restaurant, before the afternoon is spent relaxing.

We provide a range of seminars during the event, specifically for our delegates, with various local and international experts talking and answering questions about trade in and with Mexico. These discussions include HS classifications, and import and export rules.

The second full day is spent visiting local stores and malls, before heading to ANTAD and those prescheduled appointments with buyers from Mexico's largest chains. We visit some of our client booths, and then head back for the second evening seminar. Last year, this was titled, 'How to sell in Mexico', and delegates benefited from four guest speakers. After this seminar, we tend to head out to Manolos, my favorite restaurant in Guadalajara, where I've been a regular for six years.

While the third day is spent mainly in seminars, and I present the pros and cons of opening your own business in Mexico, my history of selling in and to Mexico, and my recommendations.

The final night is spent at the very best restaurant, Santo Coyote, sampling the best food and the best tequilas.

We still have a few seats left for next year's event, for more information or to request an invitation to this exclusive event, visit www.mexicosalesmadeeasy.com/ceotour

OTHER TRADE SHOWS

While I've spent a lot of time discussing ANTAD in particular, Mexico is growing at such a pace that the number of trade fairs is exploding. Here is my favorite website: http://www2.megaexpo.com/

I have included ones that have to do with food and consumer goods.

These include:

1. Expo Carnes 2015 México, Monterrey
DATE: FEB 18-20 2015
MONTERREY, NUEVO LEON, MEXICO.
Industry: Food
www.expocarnes.com/

2. EXPO PACK GUADALAJARA 2015
DATE: MARCH 18-20 2015
GUADALAJARA, JAL. MEXICO
Industry: Packaging
http://www.expopackguadalajara.com.mx

3. ALIMENTARIA MEXICO 2015
DATE: MAY 26-28 2015
Mexico City - México – Venue: Centro Banamex
http://www.alimentaria-mexico.com/

4. EXPO ANTAD
MARCH 2015
http://www.expoantad.net/expo2014/

5. EXPO CAFE & GOURMET
DATE: FEB 26- 28 2015
EXPO GUADALAJARA, MEXICO
http://www.tradex.mx/CyGGuadalajara/

6. PESCAMAR
DATE: JUNE 24, 25 and 26
PLACE: WORLD TRADE CENTER, MEXICO CITY.
SEAFOOD EXPO
www.pescamar.com.mx

7. AGROBAJA
DATE: JUNE 2015
MEXICALI, BC.
AgroBaja is the only livestock, fishery & agricultural exhibition that takes place in the borderline between Mexico and the United States
http://www.agrobaja.com/2014/AGROBAJA-2014

8. FERIA INTERNACIONAL DE FRANQUICIAS
DATE: 5-7 MARCH
WORLD TRADE CENTER, MEXICO CITY.
http://www.fif.com.mx/index_fif2013.cfm

9. CONFITEXPO 2015
DATE: AUGUST 4-7 2015
GUADALAJARA, MEXICO
http://confitexpo.com/

10. FESTIVAL DEL QUESO Y EL VINO 5a EDICIÓN
DATE: APRIL30 2015
ENSENADA, MEXICO

11. 4o FESTIVAL DEL TACO Y EL PLATILLO MEXICANO
DATE: APRIL 18 2015
ENSENADA, MEXICO
canirace@prodigy.net.mx

From experience, I can tell you that the very best results from trade shows are made when taking an active approach to this passive marketing tool. There are plenty of opportunities to exhibit and build lasting trading relationships, but these have to be managed from months before attendance at a show.

By arranging meetings in advance, and then ensuring they take place, you'll already be a step ahead of your competition. Of course, you'll also need to make sure that your stand is set up with all your advertising materials, and that these arrive in Mexico in plenty of time.

One of the biggest mistakes new companies make is thinking they don't have to 'import' sample products. Whatever products you exhibit at trade shows, will have to undergo the importation process as if they were being sold in the normal course of business.

Trade shows are not easy. To achieve the very best return on your investment you'll need to plan well in advance and use every resource at your disposal. I'd always recommend using insiders who know the people you need to talk to and will be able to arrange pre-qualified meetings.

The services we provide at Mexico Sales Made Easy have been developed over years of personal experience and specialized expertise.

Of course, exhibiting at trade shows has an intrinsic cost. This cost includes:

- Charge for stand
- Marketing materials
- Promotional costs
- Import costs
- Taxes and duties
- Administration costs

- Travel costs

Yet, even with those fixed investments, trade shows are still enormously successful if they are approached in the right way.

Even better is this: by the end of this book, I'll have let you in on the secret of how you could have the US government pay up to half of your Mexico trade show costs!

First, though, let's look at that nagging problem of the language.

CHAPTER 4

NO ES NECESARIO HABLAR ESPAÑOL
(YOU DON'T NEED TO SPEAK SPANISH)

"If we're growing, we're always going to be out of our comfort zone." – John Maxwell

¿NO HABLAS ESPAÑOL? ¡NO HAY PROBLEMA!

Conducting trade in a foreign country can be a daunting experience. Not only are the traditions and customs of doing business different, but most important is the language barrier. Selling your product in Mexico is no different. Spanish, of course, is the world's second language of business after English; more important than French, Portuguese, and Chinese.

Get your monthly Mexpert Report FREE! Go to: www.mexicosalesmadeeasy.com

When I first started doing business in Mexico, I could barely speak Spanish. But I didn't let that stop me. There are some things you will definitely need to do to get over the potential language barrier, but learning to speak perfect Spanish isn't one of them.

By the latest estimates, 90% of all Spanish top management speaks English fluently – probably better than you and I, in fact. Mexican directors and managers tend to be very well educated, elite executives, which actually makes it easier to do business, not harder.

In house requirements

I recommend you have one in-house Spanish speaker. While Mexican management is known for its ability to conduct business in English, once you're working with and supplying your buyers with your product, you'll find the administration and ordering staff are less likely to speak English.

There are also US government resources that you can utilize, but you shouldn't rely on these.

By having a Spanish-speaking staff member, you'll be able to more quickly take care of business, problems as they arise, and translate written documentation, such as emails, letters, and contracts (yes, all contracts will need to be in Spanish).

If this sounds like a new and costly item of expense if you don't currently have a Spanish-speaking member of staff, then you could always contract out this requirement. Several of our clients use part-time workers from India to undertake translation work for them, with costs as low as four dollars per hour.

When in Mexico, I have conducted business using a translation application on my cell phone. Translation programs on the internet and stand-alone software are increasing in capability and accuracy every day, too.

MEXICAN BUSINESS CULTURE

Business culture in Mexico has a lot of differences from that in the United States. If you're going to be successful, understanding how Mexican businesses operate is a useful tool. For example, whereas many US businesses now have a flattened management structure, Mexican businesses operate in a more hierarchical manner.

If you play by Mexican business rules, you'll be better received and foster a relationship that will lead to your product being bought (providing your product is good and conforms to Mexican import laws, of course).

So here are a few tips about doing business in Mexico that will help you and your product on the road to success:

Greeting etiquette

As I've said, businesses in Mexico are very hierarchical. It naturally follows that individuals like to be recognized for their status. You'll hear titles such as 'Licenciado' (graduate) and 'Ingeniero' (engineer) used.

If you're unsure of a specific title, then always address the person to whom you're speaking with Mr. (Senor) or Mrs./Miss (Senora/ Senorita) before their surname. Also, here in the U.S. most businesses have done away with the formality of surnames. In Mexico, though, it's far more accepted to use surnames until you have been invited to use first names.

You'll also find that men and women shake hands upon first meeting, though in subsequent meetings don't be surprised to be slapped on the shoulder if it's a man doing the greeting. Women are greeted with a kiss on the right cheek. When you're leaving, all of this is repeated. It can sometimes take longer to leave a meeting than it did to conduct the meeting!

Meeting etiquette

In the United States and Europe, dress code has been largely relaxed, but, again, in Mexico things are generally more formal—wearing suits and ties is a sign of respect.

Another anomaly in Mexico is that it's common for business meetings to be 'set up' by a contact that can vouch for you: this may be a mutual contact, or business associate. After the initial meeting, then it's far easier to press ahead with your new business contact.

Although Hispanic timekeeping is a relaxed affair, it is best to be on time – this is a tradition that the Mexicans are picking up from the U.S. /and continental Europe.

Be prepared for big business to be done in person: the Mexicans like to strike up a personal relationship before business is considered. Always have your business card ready. While on the subject of business cards, just like your promotional and POS materials, they should at least be in Spanish on one side.

THE LANGUAGE OF BUSINESS

You'll hear from many sources that business meetings are always conducted in Spanish. I've never found this to be the case, but it's always wise to check. Don't be afraid to take an interpreter with you, just in case.

All this said, there are approximately one hundred words that, if you learn, will help you conduct most of your business – certainly the basics.

Just like anyone, the Mexicans appreciate some effort on your part. Learning how to meet and greet in Spanish is a great start, perhaps order a coffee, and so on. A few simple phrases like this will prove your respect for the person you're meeting, and show that you really are interested in doing business.

However, while most Mexican businessmen will be happy to talk business in English, all your product manuals, marketing literature, and other written material should be in Spanish.

Another great recommendation for helping you with writing to customers in Mexico, Business Writing for Dummies, which I am a contributor for "writing to Mexico". To order visit http://www.amazon.com

100 USEFUL SPANISH WORDS

Here are the one hundred words I think you'll find most useful. Those words ending in –er, -ar, and –ir are verbs that will need to be conjugated. You'll need to practice how to put these words together, and this website will help you do so:

http://www.howdoyousay.net/english-spanish/Where_do_you_work/

Be warned about one thing: although it won't often be necessary to conduct business in Spanish, once you start speaking it and see the reaction you get simply for trying, you'll be hooked on learning more!

	SPOKEN		WRITTEN	
	English	Spanish	English	Spanish
1	a, an	uno, un	the	la
2	after	después de	of	de
3	again	otra vez	and	y
4	all	todos	a	un
5	almost	casi	to	a
6	also	también	in	en
7	always	siempre	is	es
8	and	y	you	usted
9	because	porque	that	que
10	before	antes	it	lo
11	big	grande	he	él
12	but	pero	was	fue
13	(I) can	puedo	for	para
14	(I) come	Yo vengo	on	en
15	either/or	ya sea / o	are	son
16	(I) find	me parece	as	como
17	first	primero	with	con
18	for	para	his	su
19	friend	amigo	they	ellos
20	from	de	I	yo
21	(I) go	me voy	at	en
22	good	bueno	be	ser
23	goodbye	despedida	this	este
24	happy	feliz	have	tener
25	(I) have	tengo	from	de
26	he	él	or	o
27	hello	¡Hola	one	uno
28	here	aquí	had	había
29	how	cómo	by	por
30	I	yo	word	palabra
31	(I) am	estoy	but	pero
32	if	si	not	no
33	in	en	what	¿qué
34	(I) know	sé que	all	todos

35	last	pasado	were	fueron
36	(I) like	me gusta	we	nosotros
37	little	poco	when	cuando
38	(I) love	me encanta	your	su
39	(I) make	Puedo hacer	can	puede
40	many	muchos	said	dijo
41	one	uno	there	hay
42	more	más	use	uso
43	most	más	an	un
44	much	mucho	each	cada
45	my	mi	which	que
46	new	nuevo	she	ella
47	no	no	do	hacer
48	not	no	how	cómo
49	now	ahora	their	sus
50	of	de	if	si
51	often	a menudo	will	voluntad
52	on	en	up	hasta
53	one	uno	other	otro
54	only	sólo	about	sobre
55	or	o	out	fuera
56	other	otro	many	muchos
57	our	nuestro	then	entonces
58	out	fuera	them	les
59	over	encima	these	estos
60	people	personas	so	así
61	place	lugar	some	algunos
62	please	por favor	her	su
63	same	mismo	would	se
64	(I) see	veo	make	hacer
65	she	ella	like	como
66	so	así	him	lo
67	some	algunos	into	en
68	sometimes	a veces	time	tiempo
69	still	todavía	has	ha
70	such	tal	look	ver
71	tell	decir	two	dos
72	thank you	gracias	more	más

73	that	que	write	escribir
74	the	la	go	ir
75	their	sus	see	ver
76	them	les	number	número
77	then	entonces	no	no
78	there is	hay	way	forma
79	they	ellos	could	podría
80	thing	cosa	people	personas
81	(I) think	Creo que	my	mi
82	this	este	than	de
83	time	tiempo	first	primero
84	to	a	water	de agua
85	under	bajo	been	ha
86	up	hasta	call	llamar
87	us	nosotros	who	que
88	(I) use	yo uso	oil	aceite
89	very	muy	its	su
90	we	nosotros	now	ahora
91	what	¿qué	find	encontrar
92	when	cuando	long	largo
93	where	donde	down	abajo
94	which	que	day	día
95	who	que	did	hizo
96	why	¿porqué	get	obtener
97	with	con	come	venir
98	yes	sí	made	hecho
99	you	usted	may	puede
100	your	su	part	parte

CHAPTER 5

HOW TO FIND DISTRIBUTION IN MEXICO?

There is an old story of some avid hunters who seek out and hire a highly recommended guide to lead them to hidden herds of giant elk. Guns over shoulders, they hike following the guide through woods, up mountains, through rivers, into snow, for hours and hours, until they gradually realize they've hiking in circles. "Hey" one hunter says, "you've got us lost," I thought you said you were the best hunting guide in the United States?

"I did sir," the guide said ruefully, "but I believe we are now lost in Mexico."

"In the end, all business operations can be reduced to three words; people, product and profits." Unless you've got a good team, you can't do much with the other two."

– Lee Iacocca

THE IMPORTANCE OF YOUR DISTRIBUTOR

No matter how good your product is, and your marketing efforts, it will count for nothing if you can't move your product from warehouse to point of sale. You could speak perfect Spanish, have a great marketing plan, and accept orders for thousands of units of your product, but if you can't distribute to your outlets and retailers, your reputation will be shot down in flames before it has even got off the ground.

Get your monthly Mexpert Report FREE! Go To: www.mexicosalesmadeeasy.com

If you think of your business plan as the Field Marshall of your business, and the sales and marketing plan is the General, then the distributor is your soldier on the ground. Without that soldier, your product isn't going to fly.

Not every business is the same. Each will cater to different sections of society, and even rely on different demographics for sales. You might believe these factors by themselves will dictate your choice of distributor, but you'll also need to consider other things about your product. For example, your distributor will need to have the ability to ship your product: is it heavy, bulky, fragile, hazardous, liquid, solid, or gas? Does it need to travel at a specific temperature? All of these questions, and more, need to be answered in your quest to find the right distributor.

Of course, your sales will depend upon your sales price – and when calculating this, you'll need to include the cost of distribution. There's an unbreakable link between distribution, marketing, and sales. So, you need to think about distribution early and fuse it into your business and marketing plans.

Another thing you need to consider is how your business success will be intricately linked to your distributor. You'll need a close relationship with them: your sales and profits depends every bit as much on them as their profits depend upon your marketing and sales.

With every company I've worked with, the selection of distributor has been a key element to the success of their sales in Mexico. But I've also seen mistakes made by companies who haven't taken sound advice when it comes to selection of their distributor.

THE WONDERFUL WORLD OF PRICING IN MEXICO

So here is a famous quote my good friend and partner came up with. I always remember this before I go into a sales call, it makes me chuckle.

Here goes:

"You will sit down with a buyer and he will say, "you are too expensive" now what is it that you are selling.

John Cathcart

Do not go in with your lowest price. You need to do your homework, know what discounts they will ask for and add it to your sales price.

Discounts may be for self-distribution, "Pronto Pago" (pay early), monthly promotions, new store opening, etc, etc. Do your homework or hire someone who knows this market.

FINDING THE RIGHT DISTRIBUTOR

If you have the wrong distributor, you'll never succeed in Mexico. That's a fact.

The first piece of the jigsaw puzzle is to establish exactly what you want the distributor to do for you. You need to ask questions like:

- Will you prepare all the point-of-sale marketing reports, or will the distributor?
- Will the distributor be expected to help sell your product?
- Will you need to train the distributor's salespeople?

Of course, there are plenty additional considerations to address when it comes to distributor choice. When I begin speaking to clients about the hazards of getting it wrong, the rewards of getting it right, and begin to discuss the finer details of their needs…that's when they begin to realize what an important decision distribution poses.

The main question to ask about distribution is this:

- What do your customers want?

To secure the right distribution model and the right distributor, first think about how your customers will find out about your product, search for it, and buy it. For example, if the end user is going to be buying your product from a chain store, then you need a distributer with great links to the major chain stores.

HOW DO YOU FIND THE RIGHT DISTRIBUTOR?

By now you should realize that finding a distributor is not as easy as clicking on Google and emailing the first name of search results from page one. Apart from all of the problems I've highlighted above, many Mexican companies simply aren't listed online. So you need a way to locate your ideal distributor. In a moment I'll show you the three ways to find your distributor.

Locating your own distributor, cold, is hard work, with no guarantees, as this computer manufacturer found out to Luckily there are routes you can use that have far higher success rates.

1. Take advantage of U.S. Export Agencies

US trade missions (see, for example, www.export.gov) have ambition of allowing businesses to meet directly with international partners. They can help you by:

- Setting up one-to-one meetings with governmental officials and industry executives;
- Supporting networking events with local business communities;
- Media coverage;
- Site visits;

We keep our clients informed as to the trade missions that will be of most benefit to them. We keep our clients informed as to the trade missions that will be of most benefit to them.

2. Trade Shows

There are hundreds of trade shows across Mexico every year. These cover different industries, different geographies and regions, but all have certain things in common:

- They are visited by customers
- They offer great opportunity to sell your product
- Distributors gather in numbers, looking for potential new products for their customers and distribution relationships

I've discovered how to work tradeshows in Chapter 3. They're not cheap, but can be extremely lucrative, and I speak from personal experience, as well as the experience of helping so many clients at trade shows. Let me reiterate the best approach to get the best results from trade shows:

- Plan in advance
- Understand you'll have to 'import' your exhibits – get all the paperwork correct
- Use insiders who know the people you need to talk to
- Make sure your stand is set up with all your marketing materials
- Arrange pre-qualified meetings with potential buyers and distributors

3. Let a Sales Broker find you a distributor

So far, I've looked at ways in which you can find a distributor yourself. Of course, you might decide to use a sales broker to help you in Mexico. A broker represents its clients, and their brands – it's like having an external sales agent. But it's not a catch-all relationship.

For a start, the broker won't be responsible for making sure you get paid. Sure, a broker will earn commission on sales, but you need to make sure the client is credit worthy and that you get paid. It's going to help build and sell your brand. They will find you a distributor, collect orders, and hand you the buyer. It's also possible to find brokers who will undertake extra services for you – paperwork and registration to sell your product, for example.

NATIONWIDE OR REGIONAL?

Both distributors and brokers come in many shapes and sizes. Some specialize in certain products, while some operate in certain industries and others may cover the whole country or a single city or region. You'll need to decide whether you want your distributor(s) and broker(s) to operate across the nation or on a more regional basis.

You'll need to pick a distributor, which is the right size for your needs, has the right size vehicles for your products, and has adequate warehousing. I like to think of distributors as operating at three different levels (all of which may either deliver direct to the store or to a centralized warehouse).

Level 1 Distributor

These are generally the large multi-nationals, such as Coca-Cola, for example. These distributors will have exclusive rights on their main products, but also offer distribution capability of other brands. They will visit large chains and other retailers frequently – a big advantage for distributing your product. Your accounts will be visited regularly, perhaps even daily.

The drawback is they are hard to contract, and will want to be assured your product will sell in large numbers. They also command premium rates for distribution – they may be everybody's choice, but they are also the most expensive and exclusive.

Level 2 Distributor

These medium-sized distributors might concentrate on one particular industry, or carry several different types of products. They will still cover large areas, but you'll need to support sales. You'll need to get out into the field, and use every trick possible to promote sales of your product yourself. You'll need someone on the ground, as it were.

Support this level of distributor well, and you'll see profits soar.

Level 3 Distributor

Smallest of all distributors are those at the third level. These are localized, small firms, which may only have two or three vehicles and a hundred or so accounts.

The clear disadvantage is they don't have the reach of Level 1 and Level 2 distributors. But they do have other advantages. For starters, they'll carry a limited range of products, so you won't be competing against thousands of large brands. Because of this, they'll give you a higher profile. Niche marketers find this particularly useful.

They'll also have close relationships with their customers and your accounts, though you'll still need to provide support also, incentives work very well with Level 3 distributors. You'll need to spend time to train them in your product so they know how to help you sell it and open accounts.

WHAT ALL DISTRIBUTORS WANT

Irrespective of size and scope, there are some things all distributors expect from you.

Profit

The first of these is profit. A distributor doesn't work for bread alone. They will expect your product to be good enough to sell. It will need to be marketed properly, appeal to target consumers, and retail at the right price. If it doesn't do this, then no distributor will be interested in working with you.

Marketing

The distributor won't see it as his job to chase accounts or open them for you. When your working relationship is in place and bedded down, you may find the distributor will take a more active role in account procurement – especially if your product is selling well – but it is you who will sell to retailers and support those retailers in their efforts to sell to the end consumer.

Support

Your distributor will want support from you in a number of ways. You'll need to provide training, point-of-sale materials, ride-alongs, product training, and staff incentives.

All of these criteria will likely be detailed in the contract you sign with your distributor.

ABOUT CONTRACTS

You should remember that some of your accounts might stipulate the distributor they want you to use. Irrespective of this, you'll have various options open to you for distribution of your product.

You might, for example, decide that a **warehouse program** is best for you and your retailer. This simply means your distributor will deliver to a central warehouse (operated by the retailer). This is often the case for larger retailers, such as Wal-Mart, and gives you the advantage of not needing to arrange single-store delivery. (You'll still have to support in-store sales efforts.)

Single-store delivery distribution is commonly referred to as **drop shipping**. This is slower and more labor intensive than warehouse programs, but does allow greater interaction with retailers. Of course, this also comes at a greater expense.

For successful drop shipping, you'll need effective sales mechanisms in place, and perhaps a call center and website to support your retailers.

Any contract signed with a distributor will be designed to protect both you and the distributor.

Distributors spend a lot of time, money, and effort setting up their territories. The last thing they want is competition entering and undercutting them. They want to be contracted to you to help protect their efforts and investment.

Therefore, it's common for distributors to seek exclusivity for territories with you. However, they may also work by retailer type, or by product type – it could be you may need to sign contracts with several distributors in a single territory, each serving a different retail sector – pharmacies, confectionary stores, supermarkets, convenience stores, etc.

Whatever type of contract you sign, you'll find some clauses common among them:

- Contract term
- Trademark use
- Support programs
- Termination clauses

One further point about contracts – Level 1 distributors are most likely to require exclusivity. That's fine – they have great scope, great contacts, and it's only natural they'll want to protect their interests. Level 3 distributors are the ones least likely to require a 'catch-all' contract.

CHAPTER 6

HOW TO GET $300,000 OF FREE ADVERTISING

"Success always comes when preparation meets opportunity." – Henry Hartman

THE IMPORTANCE OF GETTING YOUR NAME 'OUT THERE'

One thing I can say with almost absolute certainty is that your product is not unique. Your business is not different, they all need marketing and they all need to get their name out there.

Get your monthly Mexpert Report FREE! Go to: www.mexicosalesmadeeasy.com

The answer to tapping into these customers is all in the advertising. But, as you know, marketing and promoting your business and products is an expensive undertaking. I'm now going to let you into the world of free advertising. Well, let me be clear about this – it's not free advertising, but it's paid for by the United States Government. That's even better than free, because you're getting the U.S. government helping you to promote your goods and services!

INTRODUCING WUSATA

If your company is based in the Western United States, and produces agricultural and branded products, you're going to love WUSATA – Western United States Agricultural Trade Association.

The WUSATA program is one that many of our clients and my own companies use. They'll provide you and your company with plenty of useful information, help and guidance about exporting to Mexico. You can also access their database of market size and potential, best performing geographies, and so on. They hold educational seminars and webinars to get you up to speed and keep you informed. Apart from all of its information and educational resource, and best of all, WUSATA will help pay your advertising costs.

You see, WUSATA has been set up to promote the agriculture business of the Western United States. It wants you to succeed because when you succeed so does the region. It's a government funded body, and has extensive links to other trade associations, government agencies, and trade offices.

ARE YOU ELIGIBLE?

If you're a small to medium agribusiness, headquartered in the Western United States, and your products are at least 50% US agricultural origin (by weight and excluding packaging and added water), then you're eligible to participate in a WUSATA program.

WUSATA run two programs which will help you promote your product into Mexico. One of these is the **Generic Program**, which helps exporters through a number of trade activities which will link you with qualified buyers in Mexico. These activities include:

- Culinary training
- Education webinars and seminars
- Food service promotion
- In-store demonstrations
- Market research
- Restaurant promotions
- Technical seminars
- Trade missions
- Trade shows

Many trade shows – including ANTAD – have a WUSATA pavilion, and your product will be advertised next to others.

All this, of course, is great marketing for you and your brand, which will be instantly seen as being endorsed by a US government trade body.

The real juice, though, is in the WUSATA Branded Program.

THE WUSATA BRANDED PROGRAM

This is a great program that is really designed to help your brand awareness in Mexico. Of course, you won't be able to claim every penny of costs of advertising, but you can claim up to 50% of most of your costs.

It's not only the reimbursement of these costs that is so attractive, but the results that can be achieved with WUSATA's help. From its own figures, the average company receives a 30:1 ROI from its marketing efforts.

Compare that to the 93:1 ROI from participants in WUSATA's Branded Program. You don't only get dollars back, but you receive a higher level of recognition from your target market.

Providing your marketing promotes your brand name and the fact that its origin is in the US Western States, you can claim reimbursement on a whole host of activities, including:

- Advertising in magazines, newspapers, television, radio, billboards, etc.
- Any equipment you have had to hire for in-store demonstrations, including the space, fixtures and fittings, and display units
- Your printed sales materials, such as banners, brochures, leaflets, posters, catalogs, and pricelists
- And even the costs of repackaging for the Mexican market!

And if you are exhibiting at an approved domestic trade show, you can claim against all the above expenses for these, too. But, the good news doesn't stop here.

If you're exhibiting at international shows – such as ANTAD – then your eligible expenses will include airfare, lodging, and meals (at the pier diem rate) for two representatives, and the freight for samples shipped to promotional activities or customers. And you can claim for room and pitch rental, equipment, and printed materials, as well as:

- Demonstrators
- Translators
- Interpreters

WHAT YOU CAN'T CLAIM AGAINST

Of course, there are plenty of costs that you might associate with your advertising push that aren't eligible for reimbursements. Basically, this is anything that doesn't include your brand name and statement of US origin such as:

- Administration costs – office expenses, parking fees, business cards, etc.
- Business development costs – sponsorships, seasonal greetings cards, etc.
- Capital expenditure – equipment with a life of more than one year, building purchase, etc.

Also not eligible would be the costs of distributors, contractors, market research, in-house design and printing, and project management costs.

HOW MUCH CAN YOU REQUEST

If you're new to exporting to Mexico, then in your first year you can request reimbursement of up to $25,000. Experienced exporters see this amount rise to $50,000 in the first year.

After the first year, you can claim up to $300,000!

HOW TO APPLY FOR THE BENEFITS OF THE BRANDED PROGRAM

To take advantage of this opportunity, you'll need to apply to join the program by providing all the correct paperwork (see below) by certain dates. Your application and paperwork will be reviewed, and if approved you'll have the level of funding calculated. All the relevant dates are available here.

Any claim for reimbursement must be made no later than 90 days after the end of your marketing activity, and has to be made on a Claim Form 202. Each item that you're claiming for will need to be supported with the following paperwork:

- Invoice
- Proof of payment
- Proof of activity

WUSATA will test for fraud, authenticating products and businesses, payment and activities, as well as sources of funding.

YOUR APPLICATION – REQUIRED PAPERWORK

You can apply to join the Branded Program online (you'll need to pay a $250 non-refundable fee), supplying information about your company and your Mexico marketing plans. You'll also have to provide the following paperwork:

- Pre-Qualification Worksheet
- 2015 Application (completed original copy)
- Certification Statement (completed original copy)
- Check for $250 application fee payable to WUSATA
- One set of company and product literature
- Dun and Bradstreet Business Background Report (required for new applicants and every 2 years thereafter)
- A copy of the company's most recent Federal Tax Return as submitted to the IRS including Federal Statements and K1's (as applicable), less depreciation schedules.
- A signed Certification of Exclusivity for Brands you do not own

There is a 6% administration fee payable on the amount of your reimbursement when you sign contracts – and when you've signed these contracts and paid these fees, you're in the program!

Although this might seem a pretty paperwork-intensive process, which is true, every company I've worked with has come out the other end thankful they took the time and effort. And not just thankful, but financially far better-off.

WHAT TO DO NOW

"How I look at Opportunities, I keep saying yes, until there is a reason to say NO! Sometimes it take 15 seconds or 15 months of asking the right questions to say no."-- Sandro Piancone

The methods and strategies that I've discussed throughout this book will help you to broaden and deepen your market. International expansion is just a border away, with one of the world's fastest growing affluent societies on our doorstep.

Everything I've written about within these pages has been tried and tested and honed to perfection, first through my own companies as they expanded their business and profits throughout Mexico, and then adding in the flexibility that individual clients need.

The answer to the original question posed at the start of this book - "How will my product sell in Mexico?" – is a definite yes. Unfortunately I don't have the page space to recount all of the successes that Mexico Sales Made Easy has achieved over the years. But if you'd like to know more, please feel free to drop me an email or contact the Mexperts at www.mexicosalesmadeeasy.com

Of course, to ensure your product's success and its profits from your new Mexican customers you'll need to follow a plan and create a strategy for success. As we've seen, you don't need to speak Spanish, but you do need to know how to market and distribute in Mexico. That's where the Mexperts come in: we've seen it, done, it, helped clients, and now I've even written the book!

His office is in San Diego, California and should you wish to contact him directly about consulting, speaking, or just comment about the book please e-mail him at spiancone@mexicosalesmadeeasy.com or call his offices at (619) 616-2973.

BONUS CHAPTER

CASE STUDIES

Mexico Sales Made Easy (MSME) has been fortunate to work with some amazingly fun and successful businesses. To capture the lessons and strategies along the way, I like to interview my clients or present them as case studies as a way to help others. Below are just a few real-life accounts of what is possible when we work together to answer the question, "How Will My Product Sell in Mexico?"

VIDBOX MEXICO

Interview with Daniel Ortega, Vice President of Sales for Vidbox Mexico

MSME: What does your company do?

DANIEL: We are based in Tijuana, Mexico and with the help of MSME, we will be rolling out our business nationwide very soon. We are a ground-breaking company that carries state-of-the-art automated retail kiosks that rents movies and video games. We are taking the success of Redbox and bringing it to Mexico.

MSME: Tell us in which way did MSME help you to accomplish your goals or objectives.

DANIEL: They have done everything for us to help launch the project the easiest, fastest way possible. They first assisted us with all the legal requirements to operate these types of machines in Mexico, they handled every single legal aspect of it. They even trademarked our name Vidbox and will handle all the equipment's importations and the logistics to place every kiosk on site. Not only that, they even placed us face to face with every single buyer from the largest chain stores in the country through their "CEO Tour" that they performed just a few months ago. Where else can you meet all of the buyers in a three-day period? It was fantastic.

MSME: Were you having any trouble before you started working with MSME?

DANIEL: They showed us the ABCs to doing business in Mexico and how to apply it to our specific market, worked together with us with the minimum details on commercial, marketing, legal and logistical fields.

They developed a system that allowed us to have the kiosks in Mexico for a price almost 35% under any other custom agency quotation, and half the time to import them – which provided us with huge savings. I would highly recommend using Mexperts for any enterprise wishing to do business in Mexico, particularly if you are clueless in Mexico business culture.

If you would like more information on Vidbox, please visit www.vidbox.com.mx

QUESO NERY'S CHEESE SUCCESS

Interview with Jose Sierra, Vice President of Distribution for Queso Nery's

JOSE: We are a 30 year old cheese company that imports and distributes cheese to all of the supermarket and convenience store chains in Baja California Mexico and now launching nationwide throughout Mexico.

MSME: How did you start your journey with the Mexperts?

JOSE: Our president had worked with them in the past and knew of their experience importing cheese and needed their expertise to help launch the new products.

MSME: Tell us in which way did MSME help you to accomplish your goals or objectives.

JOSE: We were launching several new cheese lines with over 50 SKUs, and Sandro and his team did all of the trademarks, all of the NOM 51 labeling and helped with the HS classifications so we could cross the new product as quick and efficient as possible. We were amazed at the speed and professional that their staff was able to turn around the work we provide them.

MSME: Where you having any trouble before you started working with MSME?

JOSE: Yes, we always had trucks of cheese stuck at the border, now that has been a thing of the past. As for trademarks, we only had one brand, now we have several and keep adding new ones every month. They always come up with creative ways for packaging and marketing that is always fun and exciting. They showed us a way to save thousands of dollars in import permits, labeling requirements, and time (which is money) not to have cheese stuck at the border.

US TOBACCO DE MEXICO

Interview with Carlos Varela, Vice President of Private Label Distribution for US Tobacco De Mexico.

CARLOS: We are based in Tijuana, Mexico. We are an innovative tobacco company that produces private label cigarettes (made from Grade A imported USA Tobacco) for the convenience store chains and distributors (mayoristas) in Mexico.

MSME: How did you start your journey with the Mexperts?

CARLOS: I met them at at ANTAD, the largest supermarket trade show in Latin America.

MSME: Which way did MSME help you to accomplish your goals or objectives?

CARLOS: Their knowledge in the regulations for the tobacco imports like COFEPRIS, fees, taxes and logistics were the key to accelerate the process for more efficient distribution and sales in Mexico. They have also done the research and the filing of over 50 trademarks for our cigarette brands in Mexico.

MSME: It sounds like there are a lot of details that had to be handled. What obstacles did you face during the process?

CARLOS: The import of tobacco into Mexico is very complicated because of the multinational companies and the regulations get to be a headache, however MSME has the expertise in this field and has improved our process for the better. MSME played a critical role in making it happen. They took care of all of the legal and accounting laws and permits to open our first manufacturing plant in Mexico.

MSME: That sounds like a lot of work and it appears it has paid off. Can you tell us more about your upcoming plant opening?

CARLOS: Yes, it is very exciting. I did not think we would have accomplished so much in such a short time. MSME was also responsible for getting us connected with the right machine builders and manufacturing contacts that we needed.

MSME: What advice would you give our readers about starting a business in Mexico?

CARLOS: It doesn't have to be difficult as long as you find the right people to help you. It was a comfort to me to know MSME had already done what I needed to do. It is not complicated when you are guided by someone who has been where you are and knows all of the steps, and has the best contacts.

If you would like more information on US Tobacco De Mexico, please visit www.ustobaccodemexico.com

BLUE LINE FOODSERVICE DISTRIBUTION

Interview with Mathew Ilitch, President of Blue Line Foodservice Distribution

MATT: We handle the food distribution for Little Caesar's Pizza both in the USA and internationally and we are based in Farmington Hills, Michigan.

MSME: What trouble were you having with your business before contacting us?

MATT: There was no place to get complete information about how to ship to Mexico. We needed to know everything and we needed to do it without each franchise having to deal with different prices for supplies and the importing and distribution of those products.

MSME: What specifically did Mexperts do to help you?

MATT: They explained and executed the importing and distribution and helped us understand how to handle paper, supply and equipment deliveries the Little Caesar's stores throughout the country of Mexico. Now the handle the restaurant equipment logistics and now are opening a bonded warehouse which will save the franchises thousands of dollars in cash flow.

MSME: How else has Mexperts helped you do business in Mexico?

MATT: They keep us updated on new laws and regulations affecting our business in Mexico, well in advance of needing to make any changes. Their goals is to continuously improve our service to our franchisees, while lowering our costs.

If you would like more information on Blue Line Foodservice Distribution, please visit www.bluelinefd.com

How Would You Like To Make Sales Presentations To At Least 3 Of The Largest Supermarket Buyers in Mexico Without Having To Make A Single Call Or Setup A Single Meeting?

Come and join

The MEXICO CEO Tour 2015

Discover the Secret Treasure Map to selling your products in Mexico

March 17-20, 2015

Presented by

Hosted by

Sandro Piancone, Chief Mexpert Officer

Dear CEO, President, top executive or business owner looking to expand your business in Mexico!

This is your opportunity to get it _**all**_ direct from the horse's mouth; the insider tour for <u>every</u> exporter trying to sell to Mexico, fully supported with facts and data and real live examples and case histories.

I am preparing **THE most complete and detailed and valuable multi-day Training on this business that has ever been presented**. And regardless of your experience level in exporting to Mexico, I guarantee this, in your judgment, to be worth, really worth hundreds of thousands of dollars or more to you and your business.

PLEASE REQUEST A COPY OF THE PREVIEW BRIEFING WITH COMPLETE DETAILS ABOUT THE MEXICO CEO TOUR FROM THE MEXICO SALES MADE EASY OFFICE <u>IMMEDIATELY</u>.

At this writing, fewer than 12 spots remain available in Tour with spots being taken daily. Whether you are an experienced export veteran OR someone getting started or looking in and contemplating a exporting to Mexico, you should get and consider this information and this opportunity. TO REQUEST YOUR PREVIEW BRIEFING GO TO:

<u>**ceo.mexicosalesmadeeasy.com**</u>

About the Author: Sandro Piancone

Sandro is what might be called a serial entrepreneur. He started his first business at the age of ten, placing video games in retail outlets such as pizza shops, restaurants bars, and cafes for a friend of his father. The late 1970's were a great time for people in the video gaming business, and Sandro was paid $50 for each placement he made: big money back then, especially for one so young in business. Somehow, Sandro spotted the top of the market, took his profits, and moved to a more lucrative hobby and business: collecting comic books.

But that was back then. Having founded and built up several successful businesses since, he now describes himself as a 'recovering' CEO of a publicly traded foodservice company in Mexico. Sandro has introduced a number of US brands to Mexico, and helped to build them to multi-million dollar brands in the country: brand names such as Miller Beer, Thrifty Ice Cream, Roma Food, and Rockstar Energy Drinks. He sits on several corporate boards, advising on issues such as trademark and labeling requirements. Present clients include Little Caesars Pizza, Queso Nery's, Nery's Logistics, and 5-hour Energy. Since 1998, he has generated well over $500 million dollars in sales and profits for his clients and partners helping them export their products into Mexico.

He works long and hard to make sure that his clients, and their products, move to market as quickly as possible with no hiccups.

You see, in his own businesses he's made all the mistakes that could possibly have been made when transitioning from the United States to Mexico. He's had product stopped at the Mexican border because the paperwork was fouled up. But only once. He's seen his product sales hit by unfair competition issues inside Mexico. But only once. Every time he's made a mistake, he's learned from it.

It's this experience, a dedication to great customer care, and an attitude of providing flawless execution of tasks that he not only brings to Mexico Sales Made Easy, but also instills in all his staff.

While not travelling throughout Mexico, Sandro lives in San Diego with his amazing wife Kim, and his 2 cute M&Ms. He enjoys collecting rare "signed first edition" books (both comic books and auto-biographies.)

Get your monthly Mexpert Report FREE! Go to: www.mexicosalesmadeeasy.com

His office is in San Diego, California and should you wish to contact him directly about consulting, speaking, or just comment about the book please e-mail him at spiancone@mexicosalesmadeeasy.com or call his offices at (619) 616-2973.